ARIEL DORFMAN

Born in Argentina in 1942, Ariel Dorfman is a Chilean citizen. A supporter of Salvador Allende, he was forced into exile after the coup of 1973. His books have been translated into over twenty languages.

A professor at Duke University, Dorfman is a regular contributor to *The New York Times*, the *Los Angeles Times*, and *The Nation*. He lives with his wife and youngest son in Durham, North Carolina, and in Chile.

He is the author of *How to Read Donald Duck*, *The Empire's Old Clothes*, *Widows*, *The Last Song of Manuel Sendero*, *My House Is on Fire*, *Mascara*, *Last Waltz in Santiago and Other Poems of Exile and Disappearance*, *Some Write the Future*, and *Hard Rain*, as well as the award-winning plays *Widows* and *Reader*.

DEATH AND THE MAIDEN

A Play in Three Acts by
ARIEL DORFMAN

Translated from the Spanish original
LA MUERTE Y LA DONCELLA
by **Ariel Dorfman**

NICK HERN BOOKS
London

A Nick Hern Book

Death and the Maiden first published as an original paperback in
Great Britain in 1991 by Nick Hern Books

This new revised edition first published in 1994 by
Nick Hern Books Limited, 14 Larden Road, London W3 7ST

Death and the Maiden translated from the Spanish original
La Muerte y la Doncella by Ariel Dorfman

Front cover: detail from Edvard Munch's *Das Mädchen und der
Tod*, 1984, copyright Munch Museum, Oslo. Reproduced with
permission

Typeset by Country Setting, Woodchurch, Kent TN26 3TB
Printed in England by Cox & Wyman Limited, Reading, Berkshire

ISBN 1 85459 241 6

A CIP catalogue record for this book is available from
the British Library

This play is for
Harold Pinter
and María Elena Duvauchelle

Death and the Maiden was given a first reading at the Institute
for Contemporary Art in London on 30 November 1990, with:

PAULINA   Penelope Wilton
GERARDO   Michael Maloney
ROBERTO   Jonathan Hyde

Directed by Peter James

A workshop production was staged in Santiago, Chile on
10 March 1991, with:

PAULINA   Maria Elena Duvauchelle
GERARDO   Hugo Medina
ROBERTO   Tito Bustamente

Directed by Ana Reeves

Death and the Maiden had its world premiere at the Royal Court
Theatre Upstairs, on 4 July 1991, and moved to the Main Stage
at the Royal Court on 31 October 1991, with the same cast and
director:

PAULINA   Juliet Stevenson
GERARDO   Bill Paterson
ROBERTO   Michael Byrne

Directed by Lindsay Posner

The play then transferred on 11 February 1992 with the same cast
to the West End to the Duke of York's Theatre

On 20 April 1992 the cast at the Duke of York's theatre changed to:

PAULINA   Geraldine James
GERARDO   Paul Freeman
ROBERTO   Michael Byrne

On 10 August 1992 there was a further change of cast to:

PAULINA   Penny Downie
GERARDO   Danny Webb
ROBERTO   Hugh Ross

Directed by Lindsay Posner
Associate director Brian Stirner

The American Broadway premiere of *Death and the Maiden* opened at the Brooks Atkinson Theater on 17 March 1992, produced by Roger Berlind, Gladys Nederlander and Frederick Zollo, in association with Thom Mount and Bonnie Timmermann, with the following cast:

PAULINA	Glenn Close
GERARDO	Richard Dreyfuss
ROBERTO	Gene Hackman

Directed by Mike Nichols
Sets by Tony Walton
Lighting by Jules Fisher
Costumes by Ann Roth

DEATH AND THE MAIDEN

Cast of Characters

PAULINA SALAS, around forty years old

GERARDO ESCOBAR, her husband, a lawyer, around forty-five

ROBERTO MIRANDA, a doctor, around fifty

The time is the present and the place, a country that is probably Chile but could be any country that has given itself a democratic government just after a long period of dictatorship.

ACT ONE

Scene One

Sounds of the sea. After midnight. The Escobars's beach house. A terrace and an ample living/dining room where dinner is laid out on a table with two chairs. On a sideboard is a cassette recorder and a lamp. Window walls between the terrace and the front room, with curtains blowing in the wind. A door from the terrace leading to a bedroom. PAULINA Salas is seated in a chair on the terrace, as if she were drinking in the light of the moon. The sound of a faraway car can be heard. She hurriedly stands up, goes to the other room, looks out the window. The car brakes, its motor still running, the lights blasting her. She goes to the sideboard, takes out a gun, stops when the motor is turned off and she hears GERARDO's voice.

GERARDO (*voice off*). You sure you don't want to come in? Just one for the road (*Muffled reply.*) . . . Right then, we'll get together before I leave. I've gotta be back by . . . Monday. How about Sunday? (*Muffled reply.*) . . . My wife makes a margarita that will make your hair stand on end . . . I really want you to know how much I appreciate . . . (*Muffled reply.*) See you on Sunday then. (*He laughs.*)

PAULINA hides the gun away. She stands behind the curtains. The car drives off, the lights sweeping the room again. GERARDO enters.

GERARDO. Paulie? Paulina?

He sees PAULINA hidden behind the curtains. He switches on a light. She slowly comes out from the curtains.

Is that . . . ? What're you doing there like that? Sorry that I took this long to . . . I . . .

PAULINA (*trying not to seem agitated*). And who was that?

GERARDO. It's just that I . . .

PAULINA. Who was it?

GERARDO. . . . had an – no, don't worry, it wasn't anything serious. It's just that the car – luckily a man stopped – just a flat tyre. Paulina, I can't see a thing without . . .

He puts on another lamp and sees the table set.

Poor little love. It must've got cold, right, the –

PAULINA (*very calm, till the end of the scene*). We can heat it up. As long as we've got something to celebrate, that is.

Brief pause.

You do have something to celebrate, Gerardo, don't you?

GERARDO. That depends on you.

Pause. He takes an enormous nail out of his jacket pocket.

You know what this is? This is the son of a bitch that gave me a flat. And do you know what any normal man does when he gets a flat? He goes to the trunk and he gets out the spare. If the spare isn't flat too, that is. If his wife happened to remember to fix the spare, right?

PAULINA. His wife. Always got to be the wife who has to fix everything. You were supposed to fix the spare.

GERARDO. I'm really not in the mood for arguing, but we had agreed that . . .

PAULINA. You were supposed to do it. I take care of the house and you take care of –

GERARDO. You don't want help but afterwards you . . .

PAULINA. – the car at least.

GERARDO. . . . afterwards you complain.

PAULINA. I never complain.

GERARDO. This is an absurd discussion. What're we fighting about? I've already forgotten what we . . .

PAULINA. We're not fighting, darling. You accused me of not fixing your spare . . .

GERARDO. *My* spare?

PAULINA. – and I told you quite reasonably that I –

GERARDO. Hold it right there. Let's clear this thing up here and now. That you didn't fix the spare, *our* spare, that's open to discussion, but there is another little matter. The jack.

PAULINA. What jack?

GERARDO. Right. What jack? Where did you put the car jack? You know, to jack the –

PAULINA. You need a jack to hold up the car?

He embraces her.

GERARDO. Now. What the hell did you do with the jack?

PAULINA. I gave it to mother.

GERARDO (*letting go of her*). To your mother? You *gave* it to your mother?

PAULINA. Loaned it. Yes.

GERARDO. And may I ask why?

PAULINA. You may. Because she needed it.

GERARDO. Whereas I, of course, we . . . You just can't – baby, you simply cannot do this sort of thing.

PAULINA. Mom was driving down south and really needed it, while you . . .

GERARDO. While I can go fuck myself.

PAULINA. No.

GERARDO. Yes. I get a telegram and I have to leave for the city immediately to see the president in what is the most important meeting of my whole life and –

PAULINA. And?

GERARDO. . . . and this son of a bitch of a nail is lying in wait for me, fortunately not on my way there that – and there I was, without a spare and without a jack on the goddamn road.

PAULINA. I knew that you'd find someone to help you out. Was she pretty at least? Sexy?

GERARDO. I already said it was a man.

PAULINA. You said nothing of the kind.

GERARDO. Why do you always have to suppose there's a woman . . .

PAULINA. Why indeed? I just can't imagine why.

Brief pause.

Nice? The man who . . .?

GERARDO. Great guy. It's lucky for me that he . . .

PAULINA. You see? I don't know how you do it, but you always manage to fix things up so that everything turns out right for you . . . While mom, you can be sure that if she had a hat some weird person was going to stop and – you know how mom attracts the craziest sort of –

GERARDO. You can't imagine how ecstatic it makes me to think of your mother exploring the south with my jack, free of all worries, while I had to stand there for hours –

PAULINA. No exaggerating now. . .

GERARDO. Forty-five minutes. Exactly forty-five. The cars passed by as if I didn't exist. You know what I began to do? I began to move my arms around like a windmill to see if that way – we've forgotten what solidarity is in this country? Lucky for me, this man – Roberto Miranda – I invited him over for a –

PAULINA. I heard you.

GERARDO. How's Sunday?

PAULINA. Sunday's fine.

Brief pause.

GERARDO. As we're going back Monday. At least I am. And I thought you might want to come with me, shorten these holidays . . .

PAULINA. So the president named you?

Brief pause .

GERARDO. He named me.

PAULINA. The peak of your career.

GERARDO. I wouldn't call it the peak. I am, after all, the youngest of those he named, right?

PAULINA. Right. When you're minister of justice in a few years' time, that'll be the peak, huh?

GERARDO. That certainly doesn't depend on me.

PAULINA. Did you tell him that?

GERARDO. Who?

PAULINA. Your good Samaritan.

GERARDO. You mean Roberto Miranda? I hardly know the man. Besides, I haven't decided yet if I should . . .

PAULINA. You've decided.

GERARDO. I said I'd answer tomorrow, that I felt extremely honoured but that I needed . . .

PAULINA. The president? You said that to the president?

GERARDO. To the president. That I needed time to think it over.

PAULINA. I don't see what you have to think over. You've made your decision, Gerardo, you know you have. It's what you've been working for all these years, why pretend that . . .

GERARDO. Because first – first you have to say yes.

PAULINA. Well then: yes.

GERARDO. That's not the yes I need.

PAULINA. It's the only yes I've got.

GERARDO. I've heard others.

Brief pause .

If I were to accept, I must know I can count on you, that you don't feel. . . if you were to have a relapse, it could leave me . . .

PAULINA. Vulnerable, yes, it could leave you vulnerable. Stripped. You'd have to take care of me all over again.

GERARDO. That's unfair.

Brief pause.

Are you criticising me because I take care of you?

PAULINA. And that's what you told the president, that your wife might have problems with . . .

Pause.

GERARDO. He doesn't know. Nobody knows. Not even your mother knows.

PAULINA. There are people who know.

GERARDO. I'm not talking about those kinds of people. Nobody in the new government knows. I'm talking about the fact that we never made it public, as you never – as we never denounced the things that they – what they . . .

PAULINA. Only if the result was death, huh?

GERARDO. Paulina, I'm sorry, what do you –

PAULINA. This Commission you're named to. Doesn't it only investigate cases that ended in death?

GERARDO. It's appointed to investigate human rights violations that ended in death or the presumption of death, yes.

PAULINA. Only the most serious cases?

GERARDO. The idea is that if we can throw light on the worst crimes, other abuses will also come to light.

PAULINA. Only the most serious?

GERARDO. Let's say the cases that are beyond – let's say, repair.

PAULINA. Beyond repair. Irreparable, huh?

GERARDO. I don't like to talk about this, Paulina.

PAULINA. I don't like to talk about it either.

GERARDO. But we'll have to talk about it, won't we, you and I? If I'm going to spend the next few months listening to the evidence, relatives and eye-witnesses and survivors – and each time I come back home I – and you wouldn't want me to keep all that to myself. And what if you . . . if you . . .

He takes her in his arms.

If you knew how much I love you. If you knew how it still hurts me.

Brief pause.

PAULINA (*fiercely holding on to him*). Yes. Yes. Yes. Is that the yes that you wanted?

GERARDO. That's the yes that I wanted.

PAULINA. Find out what happened. Find out everything. Promise me that you'll find everything that . . . –

GERARDO. Everything. Everything we can. We'll go as far as we . . . (*Pause.*) As we're . . .

PAULINA. Allowed.

GERARDO. Limited, let's say we're limited. But there is so much we can do . . . We'll publish our conclusions. There will be an official report. What happened will be established objectively, so no one will ever be able to deny it, so that our country will never again live through the excesses that . .

PAULINA. And then?

GERARDO *is silent.*

You hear the relatives of the victims, you denounce the crimes, what happens to the criminals?

GERARDO. That depends on the judges. The courts receive a copy of the evidence and the judges proceed from there to –

PAULINA. The judges? The same judges who never intervened to save one life in seventeen years of dictatorship? Who never accepted a single habeas corpus ever? Judge Peralta who told that poor woman who had come to ask for her missing husband that the man had probably grown tired of her and run off with some other woman? That judge? What did you call him? A judge? A judge?

As she speaks, PAULINA *begins to laugh softly but with increasing hysteria.*

GERARDO. Paulina, Paulina. That's enough. Paulina.

He takes her in his arms. She slowly calms down.

Silly. Silly girl, my baby.

Brief pause.

And what would have happened if you'd had the flat? You there on that road with the cars passing, the lights passing like a train, screaming by, and nobody stopping, did you think of what could have happened to you if you found yourself alone there on the road all of a –

PAULINA. Someone would have stopped. Probably that same – Miranda?

GERARDO. Probably. Not everybody's a son of a bitch.

PAULINA. No . . . Not everybody.

GERARDO. I invited him for a drink on Sunday. What do you think?

PAULINA. Sunday's fine.

Brief pause.

I was frightened. I heard a car. When I looked it wasn't yours.

GERARDO. But there was no danger.

PAULINA. No.

Brief pause.

Gerardo.

You already said yes to the president, didn't you? The truth, Gerardo. Or are you going to start your work on the Commission with a lie?

GERARDO. I didn't want to hurt you.

PAULINA. You told the president you accepted, didn't you? Before you asked me? Didn't you? I need the truth, Gerardo.

GERARDO. Yes. I told him I'd do it. Yes. Before asking you.

Lights go down.

Scene Two

One hour later. Nobody on stage. Only the moonlight, weaker than before, coming in through the windows. Dinner has been cleared away. Sound of the sea beyond. The sound of a car approaching. Then the headlights light up the living room, are switched off, a car door is opened and closed. Someone knocks on the door, first timidly, then more strongly. A lamp is switched on from offstage and is immediately switched off. The knocking on the door gets more insistent. GERARDO *comes into the living room in his pyjamas from the bedroom.*

GERARDO (*to* PAULINA, *who is offstage*). I'm telling you – nothing is going to – all right, all right, love, I'll be careful.

GERARDO *switches on the lamp.*

I'm coming, I'm coming.

He goes to the door and opens it. ROBERTO MIRANDA *is outside.*

Oh, it's you. God, you scared the shit out of me.

ROBERTO. I'm really so sorry for this – intrusion. I thought you'd still be up celebrating.

GERARDO. You must excuse my . . . – do come in.

ROBERTO *enters the house.*

It's just that we still haven't got used to it.

ROBERTO. Used to it?

GERARDO. To democracy. That someone knocks on your door at midnight and it's a friend and not . . . –

PAULINA *edges out onto the terrace from where she will be able to hear the men but not see or be seen by them.*

ROBERTO. And not one of these bastards?

GERARDO. And my wife has . . . She's been a bit nervous and . . . So you'll understand that – you'll have to forgive her if she doesn't . . . And if we lower our voices a little . . .

ROBERTO. Of course, of course, it's my fault, I just thought .

GERARDO. Please sit down, please do . . .

ROBERTO. . . . that I'd stop by for a short visit to . . . Okay, but just a minute, no more than – but you must be asking yourself why this sudden visit . . . Well, I was driving back to my beach house.

GERARDO. Excuse me, would you like a drink? Sunday you can have one of my wife's famous margaritas, but I do possess a cognac from the duty free that I –

PAULINA *edges nearer and listens.*

ROBERTO. No, thanks, I . . . Well, a teensy-weensy bit. So I'm listening to the radio in my car and . . . all of a sudden, it hit me. I heard your name on the news, the list of names the president's chosen for his Investigating Commission, and they say Gerardo Escobar, and I said to myself that sounds familiar, but where, who, and it kept going round in my head, and when I reached our house I realised who it was. And I also remembered we'd put your spare tyre in the trunk of my car and that tomorrow you'd need it patched up and also . . . the real real truth is, you want to know the truth?

GERARDO. I can't wait.

ROBERTO. I thought to myself – this man is doing something really essential for the honour of the nation – so the country can shut the door on the divisions and hatreds of the past and I thought here's the last weekend that he's going to be free of worries for – for who knows how many months, right, because you're going to have to go up and down this country of ours listening to thousands of people . . . Don't tell me that –

GERARDO. That's certainly true, but I wouldn't go so far as to –

ROBERTO. So I thought the least I can do is drive over and leave him his spare so he won't have to go out to phone for a taxi or a tow truck – I mean, who has a phone out here.

GERARDO. You're making me feel as if I were –

ROBERTO. No, I am telling you, and this is said straight from the heart, this Commission is going to help us close an exceptionally painful chapter in our history, and here I am, alone this weekend, we've all got to help out – it may be a teensy-weensy gesture but –

GERARDO. Tomorrow would have been fine.

ROBERTO. Tomorrow? You manage to get to your car – no spare. Then you have to set out and find me. No, my friend, – and then I thought I might as well offer to go fix it with you tomorrow with my jack – which reminds me – what happened to your jack, did you find out what –

GERARDO. My wife loaned it to her mother.

ROBERTO. To her mother?

GERARDO. You know women. . .

ROBERTO (*laughing*). All too well. The last mystery. We are going to explore all the frontiers, my friend, and we will still have that unpredictable female soul. You know what Nietzsche once wrote – at least I think it was Nietzsche? That we can never entirely possess that female soul. Or maybe it wasn't him. Though you can be sure that old Nietzsche would have if he'd found himself on a weekend road without a jack.

GERARDO. And without a spare.

ROBERTO. And without a spare. Which clinches it – I really must go with you and we'll clean up the whole operation in one morning . . .

GERARDO. I feel that I am imposing.

ROBERTO. I won't hear another word. I happen to like to help people, – I'm a doctor, I told you, didn't I? But don't get it in your head that I only help important people.

GERARDO. If you had known what you were getting into you'd have stomped the accelerator to the floor, huh?

ROBERTO (*laughing*). Through the floor. No, seriously, it's no trouble at all. In fact, it's an honour. In fact, if you want to know the real real truth, look, that's why I came here tonight, to congratulate you, to tell you that . . . You are exactly what this country needs, to be able to find out the truth once and for all . . .

GERARDO. What the country needs is justice, but if we can determine at least part of the truth . . .

ROBERTO. Just what I was about to say. Even if we can't put these people on trial, even if they're covered by this amnesty they gave themselves – at least their names can be published.

GERARDO. Those names are to be kept secret. The Commission is not supposed to identify the authors of crimes or –

ROBERTO. In this country everything finally comes out into the open. Their children, their grandchildren, is it true that you did this, you did what they're accusing you of, and they'll have to lie. They'll say it's slander, it's a communist conspiracy, some such nonsense, but the truth will be written all over them, and their children, their very own children, will feel sorrow for them, disgust and sorrow. It's not like putting them in jail, but . . .

GERARDO. Maybe some day . . .

ROBERTO. Maybe if the citizens of this country get angry enough we may even be able to revoke the amnesty.

GERARDO. You know that's not possible.

ROBERTO. I'm for killing the whole bunch of them, but I can see that . . . –

GERARDO. I hate to disagree, Roberto, but in my opinion the death penalty has never solved any of the –

ROBERTO. Then we're going to have to disagree, Gerardo. There are people who simply don't deserve to be alive, but what I was really getting at was that you're going to have quite a problem . .

GERARDO. More than one. For starters, the Army is going to fight the Commission all the way. They've told the president this investigation was an insult, and dangerous, yes, dangerous, for the new government to be opening old wounds. But the president went ahead anyway, thank God, for a moment I thought he'd get cold feet, but we all know these people are ready to jump on us at the slightest mistake we make . . .

ROBERTO. Well, that was exactly my point, when you said that the names wouldn't be known, published, when you – maybe you're right, maybe we'll finally never know who these people really were, they form a sort of . . .

GERARDO. Mafia.

ROBERTO. Mafia, yes, a secret brotherhood, nobody gives out names and they cover each others' backs. The Armed Forces aren't going to allow their men to give testimony to your Commission and if you people call them in they'll just ignore your summons, just say fuck you. Maybe you're right and this thing about the children and the grandchildren is nothing but a fantasy. It may not be as easy as I thought, that's what I was really getting at.

GERARDO. Not that difficult either. The president told me – and this stays between us, of course –

ROBERTO. Of course.

GERARDO. The President told me that there are people who are ready to make statements, just so long as their confidentiality is guaranteed. And once people start talking, once the confessions begin, the names will pour out like water. Like you said: in this country we end up knowing everything.

ROBERTO. I wish I could share your optimism. I'm afraid there are things we'll never know.

GERARDO. We're limited, but not that limited. At the very least we can expect some sort of moral sanction, that's the least . . . As we can't expect justice from the courts . . .

ROBERTO. I hope to God you're right. But it's getting late. Lord, it's two o'clock. Look, I'll be back to pick you up tomorrow, let's say at – how about nine?

GERARDO. Why don't you stay over unless you've got someone waiting for you back at your . . .

ROBERTO. Not a soul.

GERARDO. Well, if you're alone.

ROBERTO. Not alone. My wife and kids have gone off to her

mother's of all places and as I hate to fly, and I've got some patients that –

GERARDO. Not at your beach house you don't. So why don't you – ?

ROBERTO. It's very kind of you but I like being by myself, watching the waves, listening to my music. Look, I came to help, not to be a bother. I'll be back tomorrow, say at –

GERARDO. I won't hear of it. You're staying. You're what? You're half an hour away?

ROBERTO. It's around forty minutes by the coast road, but if I –

GERARDO. Not another word. Paulina will be delighted. You'll see the breakfast she'll make for us.

ROBERTO. Now that convinced me. Breakfast! I don't think we even have milk at our beach house. And the real real truth is that I am incredibly tired . . .

PAULINA quickly returns, through the terrace, to her bedroom.

GERARDO. I wonder if there's anything else you might . . . ? A toothbrush is really the only thing I think I can't offer you . . .

ROBERTO. Of the two things you never share, my friend, one is your toothbrush.

GERARDO. Right!

ROBERTO. Good night.

Both GERARDO and ROBERTO exit in different directions to their respective bedrooms. A brief pause: silence and moonlight.

GERARDO (*voice off*). Paulina, love . . . That doctor who helped me out on the road, he's staying the night. Love? He's staying because tomorrow he's going to help me pick up the car. Darling, are you listening?

PAULINA (*off, as if half-asleep*). Yes, my love.

GERARDO (*voice off*). He's a friend. So don't be scared. Tomorrow you can make us a nice breakfast . . .

Only the sound of the sea in the semi-darkness.

Scene Three

A short time later. A cloud passes over the moon. The sound of the sea grows, then recedes. Silence.

PAULINA *comes into the living room.*

By the light of the moon she can be seen going to the drawer and taking out the gun. And some vague articles of clothing which appear to be stockings.

She crosses the living/dining room to the entrance to ROBERTO's *bedroom. She waits for an instant, listening. She goes into the bedroom. A few moments pass. We hear a confusing, muffled sound, followed by a sort of cry. Then silence.*

In the half-light we see her come out of the room. She goes back to her own bedroom door. She opens it, takes a key from the inside of the door, locks it. She returns to the spare bedroom. We see her dragging something in, which resembles a body but we can't be sure. As the scene continues, it can be seen that it is a body. She moves a chair and hoists the body onto it, ties it to the chair. She goes into the spare room, returns with what seems to be ROBERTO's *jacket, takes a set of car keys rom it. She starts to leave the house. Stops. Turns back to look at the body which is now clearly that of* ROBERTO. *She takes off her panties, stuffs it into* ROBERTO's *mouth.*

PAULINA *leaves the house. We hear the sound of* ROBERTO's *car. When the car's headlights are turned on, they sweep the scene and that stark brutal shot of light clearly reveals* ROBERTO *Miranda tied with ropes to one of the chairs, totally unconscious, and with his mouth gagged. The car leaves. Darkness.*

Scene Four

Before dawn. ROBERTO *opens his eyes. He tries to get up and realises that he is tied . He begins to roll over and desperately tries to free himself.* PAULINA *is sitting in front of him with her gun.* ROBERTO *looks at her with a terrorised expression in his eyes.*

PAULINA (*very calm*). Good morning, Doctor. . . Miranda, isn't it? Doctor Miranda.

She shows him the gun and points it playfully in his direction.

I had a chum from the university, name of Miranda, Ana Maria Miranda, you wouldn't be related to the Mirandas of San

Esteban, would you? She had quite a mind. A marvellous retentive memory, we used to call her our little encyclopedia. I have no idea what became of her. She probably finished her medical studies, became a doctor, just like you.

I didn't get my diploma ... I didn't get too far with my studies, Doctor Miranda. Let's see if you can guess why I didn't get my diploma, I'm pretty sure that it won't take a colossal effort of the imagination on your part to guess why.

Luckily there was Gerardo. He was – well, I wouldn't exactly say he was waiting for me – but let's say that he still loved me, so I never had to go back to the university. Lucky for me, because I felt a – well, phobia wouldn't be the right word, a certain apprehension – about medicine. I wasn't so sure about my chosen profession. But life is never over till it's over, as they say. That's why I'm wondering whether it might not be a good idea to sign up again – you know, ask that I be readmitted. I read the other day, now that the military aren't in charge anymore, that the university has begun to allow the students who were kicked out to apply for readmittance.

But here I am chatting away when I'm supposed to make breakfast, aren't I, a nice breakfast? Now you like – let's see, ham sandwiches, wasn't it? Ham sandwiches with mayonnaise. We haven't got mayonnaise, but we do have ham. Gerardo also likes ham. I'll get to know your other tastes. Sorry about the mayonnaise. I hope you don't mind that this must remain, for the moment, a monologue. You'll have your say, Doctor, you can be sure of that. I just don't want to remove this – gag, you call it, don't you? – at least not till Gerardo wakes up. But I should be getting him up. Did I tell you I phoned the garage from the pay phone? They'll be here soon.

She goes to the bedroom door, unlocks it, opens it.

The real real truth is that you look slightly bored.

Takes a cassette out of her pocket.

I took this out of your car – I took the liberty – what if we listen to some Schubert while I make breakfast, a nice breakfast, Doctor? *Death and the Maiden?*

She puts it into the cassette player. We begin to hear Schubert's quartet Death and the Maiden.

D'you know how long it's been since I last listened to this quartet? If it's on the radio, I turn it off, I even try not to go out much, though Gerardo has all these social events he's got to attend and if they ever name him minister we're going to live running around shaking hands and smiling at perfect strangers, but I always pray they won't put on Schubert. One night we were dining with – they were extremely important people, and our hostess happened to put Schubert on, a piano sonata, and I thought, do I switch it off or do I leave, but my body decided for me, I felt extremely ill right then and there and Gerardo had to take me home, so we left them there listening to Schubert and nobody knew what had made me ill, so I pray they won't play that anywhere I go, any Schubert at all, strange isn't it, when he used to be, and I would say, yes I really would say, he's still my favourite composer, such a sad, noble sense of life. But I always promised myself a time would come to recover him, bring him back from the grave so to speak, and just sitting here listening to him with you I know that I was right, that I'm – so many things that are going to change from now on, right? To think I was on the verge of throwing my whole Schubert collection out, crazy!

(*Raising her voice, to* GERARDO.) Isn't this quartet marvellous, my love?

(*To* ROBERTO.) And now I'll be able to listen to my Schubert again, even go to a concert like we used to. Did you know that Schubert was homosexual? But of course you do, you're the one who kept repeating it over and over again while you played *Death and the Maiden*. Is this the very cassette, Doctor, or do you buy a new one every year to keep the sound pure?

GERARDO *enters from the bedroom, still sleepy.*

Good morning, my darling. Sorry breakfast isn't ready yet.

Upon seeing GERARDO, ROBERTO *makes desperate efforts to untie himself.* GERARDO *watches the scene with total astonishment.*

GERARDO. Paulina! What is this? What in the name of . . . Roberto . . . Doctor Miranda.

He moves toward ROBERTO.

PAULINA. Don't touch him.

GERARDO. What?

PAULINA (*threatening him with the gun*). Don't touch him.

GERARDO. What the hell is going on here, what kind of madness is –

PAULINA. It's him.

GERARDO. Put . . . put that gun down.

PAULINA. It's him.

GERARDO. Who?

PAULINA. It's the doctor.

GERARDO. What doctor?

PAULINA. The doctor who played Schubert.

GERARDO. The doctor who played Schubert.

PAULINA. That doctor.

GERARDO. How do you know?

PAULINA. The voice.

GERARDO. But weren't you – you told me – what you told me
was all through those weeks . . .

PAULINA. Blindfolded, yes. But I could still hear.

GERARDO. You're sick.

PAULINA. I'm not sick.

GERARDO. You're sick.

PAULINA. All right then, I'm sick. But I can be sick and
recognise a voice. Besides, when we lose one of our faculties,
the others compensate, they get sharper. Right, Doctor
Miranda?

GERARDO. A vague memory of someone's voice is not proof of
anything, Paulina, it is not incontrovertible –

PAULINA. It's his voice. I recognised it as soon as he came in
here last night. The way he laughs. Certain phrases he uses.

GERARDO. But that's not . . .

PAULINA. It may be a teensy-weensy thing, but it's enough for
me. During all these years not an hour has passed that I haven't
heard it, that same voice, next to me, next to my ear, that voice
mixed with saliva, you think I'd forget a voice like his?

Imitating the voice of ROBERTO, *then of a man.*

'Give her a bit more. This bitch can take a bit more. Give it to
her.'

'You sure, Doctor? What if the cunt dies on us?'

'She's not even near fainting. Give it to her, up another notch. '

GERARDO. Paulina, I'm asking you to please give me that gun.

PAULINA. No.

GERARDO. While you point it at me, there is no possible
dialogue.

PAULINA. On the contrary, as soon as I stop pointing it at you, all dialogue will automatically terminate. If I put it down you'll use your strength to win the argument.

GERARDO. Paulina, I want you to know that what you are doing is going to have serious consequences.

PAULINA. Serious, huh? Irreparable, huh?

GERARDO. Yes, it could be – irreparable. Doctor Miranda, I have to ask your forgiveness for – my wife has been –

PAULINA. Don't you dare ask forgiveness from that piece of shit. Do you see that hand, that hand over there –

GERARDO. Untie him, Paulina.

PAULINA. No.

GERARDO. Then I will.

He moves toward ROBERTO. *Suddenly, a shot from* PAULINA*'s gun rings out. It's clear that she does not know how to fire the weapon, because she is as surprised as both men are, recoiling from the shot.* GERARDO *takes a step backward and* ROBERTO *looks desperate.*

GERARDO. Don't shoot, Paulie. Don't shoot that thing off again. Give me that gun.

Silence.

You can't do this.

PAULINA. When are you going to stop telling me what I can and can't do. 'You can't do this, you can do that, you can't do this.' I did it.

GERARDO. You did this to this man, whose only fault that we know of – the only thing you can accuse him of in front of a judge –

PAULINA *laughs derisively.*

– yes, a judge, yes, however corrupt, venal, cowardly – the only thing you could accuse him of is of stopping on the road to help someone who was in trouble, and bring me home and then offer to –

PAULINA. I almost forgot. The man from the garage will be here any minute.

GERARDO. What?

PAULINA. When I went to hide your good Samaritan's car early this morning, I stopped at a public phone and let them know we need them early. So you better get dressed. They must be about to arrive.

GERARDO. Please, Paulina, could we start being reasonable, start acting as if –

PAULINA. You be reasonable. They never did anything to you.

GERARDO. They did things, of course they did things – but we're not competing for some horror prize here, damn it – let's try and be reasonable. Even if this man was the doctor of those terrible events – he isn't, there's no reason why he should be, but let's say he was – even in that case, what right do you have to bind him like this, baby, look at what you're doing, Paulina, think of the consequences of –

The motor of a truck is heard outside. PAULINA runs to the door, half opens it and shouts out.

PAULINA. He's coming, he's coming.

She shuts the door, locks it, closes the curtains and looks at GERARDO.

Get dressed, quick. It's the tow truck. The spare's outside. I also took his jack.

GERARDO. You're stealing his jack?

PAULINA. That way mother can keep ours.

Brief pause.

GERARDO. Have you thought I could go to the police?

PAULINA. I doubt you'd do that. You believe too much in your own powers of persuasion. Besides you know that if the police do show their noses here I'll put a bullet straight through this man's head. You do know that, don't you? And then I'll put the gun in my mouth and pull the trigger.

GERARDO. Oh my baby, my baby. You're – unrecognisable. How can you possibly be this way, talk this way?

PAULINA. Explain to my husband, Doctor Miranda, what you did to me so I would be this – crazy.

GERARDO. Paulina. I want you to tell me exactly what it is you intend to do?

PAULINA. Not me. You and me. We're going to put him on trial, Gerardo, this doctor. Right here. Today. You and me. Or is your famous Investigating Commission going to do it?

Lights go down.

End of Act One

ACT TWO

Scene One

Midday. ROBERTO *is still in the same position,* PAULINA *with her back to him, looking outward to the window and the sea, rocking herself gently as she speaks to him.*

PAULINA. And when they let me go – d'you know where I went? I couldn't go home to my parents – they were so pro-military that at that time I had broken off all diplomatic relations with them, I'd see mother only once in a long while . . . Isn't this bizarre, that I should be telling you all this as if you were my confessor, when there are things I've never told Gerardo, or my sister, certainly not my mother. She'd die if she knew what I've really got in my head. Whereas I can tell you exactly what I feel, what I felt when they let me go. That night . . . well, you don't need me to describe what state I was in, you gave me a quite thorough inspection before I was released, didn't you? We're rather cosy here, aren't we, like this? Like two old pensioners sitting on a bench in the sun.

ROBERTO *makes a gesture, as if he wanted to speak or untie himself.*

Hungry? Things aren't that bad. You'll just have to be patient until Gerardo comes.

Imitating a man's voice.

'You hungry? You wanna eat? I'll give you something to eat, sweet cunt, I'll give you something big and filling so you can forget you're hungry.'

Her own voice.

You don't know anything about Gerardo, do you? – I mean you never knew a thing. I never breathed his name. Your – your colleagues, they'd ask me, of course. 'With that twat, little lady, don't tell me you haven't got someone to fuck you, huh? Come on, just tell us who's been fucking you, little lady.' But I never gave them Gerardo's name. Strange how things turn out. If I had mentioned Gerardo, he wouldn't have been named to any Investigating Commission, but would have been one of the names that some other lawyer was investigating. And I would be in front of that Commission to tell them how I met Gerardo – in fact I met him just after the military coup, helping people seek asylum in embassies – saving lives with Gerardo, smuggling people out of the country so they wouldn't be killed. I was wild and fearless, willing to do anything, I can't believe that I didn't have an ounce of fear in my whole body at that time. But I am really getting off target. That night they let me go, well, I went to Gerardo's house, I knocked on the door, over and over, just like you did last night, and when Gerardo finally answered, he looked agitated, his hair was dishevelled –

The sound of a car outside. Then a car door opening and closing. PAULINA *goes to the table and takes the gun in her hand.* GERARDO *enters.*

How did it go? Was the flat easy to fix?

GERARDO. Paulina, you are going to listen to me.

PAULINA. Of course I'm going to listen to you. Haven't I always listened to you?

GERARDO. I want you to sit down and I want you to really listen to me.

PAULINA *sits down.*

You know that I have spent a good part of my life defending the law. If there was one thing that revolted me in the past regime –

PAULINA. You can call them fascists . . .

GERARDO. Don't interrupt. If something revolted me about them it was that they accused so many men and women, that they forged evidence and ignored evidence and did not give the accused any chance of defending themselves, so even if this man committed genocide on a daily basis, he has the right to defend himself.

PAULINA. But I have no intention of denying him that right, Gerardo. I'll give you all the time you need to speak to your client, in private. I was just waiting for you to come back, that's all, so we could begin this in an orderly official fashion.

She gestures to GERARDO, *who takes the gag off* ROBERTO. *Then she indicates the cassette recorder.*

You should know, Doctor, that everything you say will be recorded here.

GERARDO. My God, Paulina, shut up! Let him say what he . . .

Brief pause. PAULINA *switches on the recorder.*

ROBERTO (*coughs, then in a rough, hoarse voice*). Water.

GERARDO. What?

PAULINA. He wants water, Gerardo.

GERARDO *rushes to fill a glass with water and brings it to* ROBERTO, *giving it to him to drink.* ROBERTO *drinks it down noisily.*

PAULINA. Nothing like good fresh water, eh, Doctor? Beats drinking your own piss.

ROBERTO. Escobar. This is inexcusable. I will never forgive you as long as I live.

PAULINA. Hold on, hold on. Stop right there, Doctor. Let's see if this thing is working.

She presses some buttons and then we hear ROBERTO'*s voice.*

ROBERTO'S VOICE FROM THE CASSETTE. Escobar. This is inexcusable. I will never forgive you as long as I live.

PAULINA'S VOICE FROM THE CASSETTE. Hold on, hold on. Stop right there, Doctor. Let's see.

PAULINA *stops the recorder.*

PAULINA. Ready. It's recording everything marvellously. We already have a statement about forgiveness. It is Doctor Miranda's opinion that it is inexcusable – that he could never forgive as long as he lives – tying someone up for a few hours, holding that person without the right to speak for a few hours. Agreed. More?

She presses another button.

ROBERTO. I do not know you, madam. I have never seen you before in my life. But I can tell you this: you are extremely ill, almost prototypically schizoid. But you, Escobar, you, sir, are not ill. You're a lawyer, a defender of human rights, a man who has been persecuted by the former military government, as I was myself, and your case is different, you are responsible for what you do and what you must do is untie me immediately. And I want you to know that every minute that passes makes you more of an accomplice to this abuse and that you will therefore have to pay the consequences of –

PAULINA (*puts the gun to his temple*). Who are you threatening?

ROBERTO. I wasn't –

PAULINA. Threatening, yes you were. Let's get this clear, Doctor. Threat time is over. Out there you bastards may still give the orders, but in here, for now, I'm in command. Now is that clear?

ROBERTO. I've got to go to the bathroom.

PAULINA. Piss or shit?

GERARDO. My God, Paulina! Doctor Miranda, she has never spoken like this in her life.

PAULINA. The Doctor's used to this sort of language . . . Come on, Doctor. Front or rear?

ROBERTO. Standing up.

PAULINA. Untie his legs, Gerardo. I'll take him.

GERARDO. Of course not. I'll take him.

PAULINA. I'll do it. Don't look at me like that. It's not as if it's the first time he's going to take his – instrument out in front of me, Gerardo. Come on, Doctor. Stand up. I don't want you pissing all over my rug.

GERARDO *unties the legs. Slowly, painfully,* ROBERTO *limps towards the bathroom, with* PAULINA *sticking the gun in his back.* GERARDO *turns off the cassette recorder.* PAULINA *goes out with* ROBERTO. *After a few instants, we can hear the sounds of urination and then flushing. Meanwhile,* GERARDO *has been pacing nervously.* PAULINA *returns with* ROBERTO.

PAULINA. Tie him up again.

GERARDO *begins to tie up* ROBERTO'*s legs.*

Tighter, Gerardo!

GERARDO. Paulina, this is intolerable. I must talk with you.

PAULINA. And who's stopping you?

GERARDO. Alone.

PAULINA. Why? The doctor used to discuss everything in my presence, they –

GERARDO. Dear, dear Paulie, please, don't be so difficult. I want to talk to you where we have some privacy.

GERARDO *and* PAULINA *go out onto the terrace. During their conversation,* ROBERTO *slowly manages to loosen his leg bonds.*

What are you trying to do? What are you trying to do, woman, with these insane acts?

PAULINA. I already told you – put him on trial.

GERARDO. Put him on trial, what does that mean, put him on trial? We can't use their methods. We're different. To seek vengeance in this fashion is not –

PAULINA. This is not vengeance. I'm giving him all the guarantees he never gave me. Not one, him and his – colleagues.

GERARDO. And his – colleagues – are you going to kidnap them and bring them here and tie them up and . . .

PAULINA. I'd have to know their names for that, wouldn't l?

GERARDO. – and then you re going to . . .

PAULINA. Kill them? Kill him? As he didn't kill me, I think it wouldn't be fair to –

GERARDO. It's good to know that, Paulina, because you would have to kill me too, I'm warning you that if you intend to kill him, you're going to have to kill me first.

PAULINA. Would you mind calming down? I haven't the slightest intention of killing him. And certainly not you . . . But as usual, you don't believe me.

GERARDO. But then, what are you going to do to him? With him? You're going to – what? What are you going to – and all this because fifteen years ago someone . . .

PAULINA. Someone what? . . . what did they do to me, Gerardo. Say it.

Brief pause.

You never wanted to say it. Say it now. They . . .

GERARDO. If you didn't say it, how was I going to?

PAULINA. Say it now.

GERARDO. I only know what you told me that first night, when . . .

PAULINA. They . . .

GERARDO. They . . .

PAULINA. Tell me, tell me.

GERARDO. They – tortured you. Now you say it.

PAULINA. They tortured me. And what else? What else did they do to me, Gerardo?

GERARDO *goes to her, takes her in his arms.*

GERARDO (*whispering to her*). They raped you.

PAULINA. How many times?

GERARDO. More than once.

PAULINA. How many times?

GERARDO. You never said. I didn't count, you said.

PAULINA. It's not true.

GERARDO. What's not true?

PAULINA. That I didn't count. I always kept count. I know how many times.

Brief pause.

And that night, Gerardo, when I came to you, when I told you, when I started to tell you, what did you swear you'd do to them when you found them? 'Some day, my love, we're going to put these bastards on trial. Your eyes will be able to rove' – I remember the exact phrase, because it seemed, poetic – 'your eyes will be able to rove over each one of their faces while they listen to your story. We'll do it, you'll see that we will.' So now, darling, tell me who do I go to now?

GERARDO. That was fifteen years ago.

PAULINA. Tell me who's supposed to listen to my accusations against this doctor, who, Gerardo? Your Commission?

GERARDO. *My* Commission? What Commission? Thanks to you, we may not even be able to investigate all the other crimes that – And I'm going to have to resign.

PAULINA. Always so melodramatic. Your brow gets all furrowed up with wrinkles that make you look ten years older. And then people will see your photograph in the newspaper and won't believe that you're the youngest member of the Commission.

GERARDO. Are you deaf? I just told you I'm going to have to resign.

PAULINA. I don't see why.

GERARDO. You don't see why, but all the rest of the country will see why, especially those who don't want any kind of investigation of the past will see why. A member of the president's Commission, who should be showing exemplary signs of moderation and equanimity –

PAULINA. We're going to suffocate from so much equanimity!

GERARDO. – and objectivity, that this very person has allowed an innocent human being to be bound and tormented in his house – do you know how the newspapers that served the dictatorship, do you know how they'll use this episode to undermine and perhaps even destroy the Commission?

Brief pause.

Do you want these people back in power? You want to scare them so they come back to make sure we don't harm them? You want the times back when these people decided our life and our death? Because if that's what you want, that's what you're going to get. Free the man, Paulina. Apologise for the mistake and free him. I've spoken to him, politically he seems to be a man we can trust or so it –

PAULINA. Oh, my little man, you do fall for every trick in the book, don't you? Gerardo, you have my promise, as solemn as it can be, that this private trial will not affect you or the Commission. Do you really think I'd do anything to trouble the Commission, stop you from finding out where the bodies of the missing prisoners are, how people were executed, where they're buried. But the members of the Commission only deal with the dead, with those who can't speak. And I can speak – it's been years since I murmured even a word, I haven't opened my mouth to even whisper a breath of what I'm thinking, years living in terror of my own . . . but I'm not dead, I thought I was but I'm not and I can speak, damn it – so for God's sake let me have my say and you go ahead with your Commission and believe me when I tell you that none of this is going to be made public.

GERARDO. Even in that case – I have to resign no matter what, and the sooner, the better.

PAULINA. You'd have to resign even if no one knew about this?

GERARDO. Yes.

PAULINA. Because of your mad wife, who was mad because she stayed silent and is now mad because she can speak?

GERARDO. Among other reasons, yes, that's so, if the truth still matters to you.

PAULINA. The real real truth, huh?

Brief pause.

Could you wait just a sec.

She goes into the other room and discovers ROBERTO *about to free himself. When he sees her, he stops immediately.* PAULINA *ties him up again, while her voice assumes male tones.*

'Hey, don't you like our hospitality? Want to leave so soon, bitch? You're not going to have such a good time outside as you're having with me, sweetie. Tell me you'll miss me. At least tell me that.'

PAULINA *begins to slowly pass her hands up and down* ROBERTO'*s body, almost as if she were caressing it. Then she goes back to the terrace.*

PAULINA. It's not only the voice I recognise, Gerardo. I also recognise the skin. And the smell. Gerardo. I recognise his skin.

Brief pause.

Suppose I was able to prove beyond a shadow of a doubt that this doctor of yours is guilty? Would you want me to set him free anyway?

GERARDO. Yes. If he's guilty, more reason to set him free. Don't look at me like that. Imagine what would happen if everyone acted like you did. You satisfy your own personal passion, you punish on your own, while the other people in this country with scores of other problems who finally have a chance to solve some of them, those people can just go screw themselves – the whole return to democracy can go screw itself –

PAULINA. Nobody's going to get screwed! Nobody's even going to know!

GERARDO. The only way to be absolutely sure about that is to kill him and in that case you're the one who's going to get screwed and I'm going to get screwed along with you. Let him go, Paulina. For the good of the country, for our own good.

PAULINA. And me? What I need? Look at me, look at me!

GERARDO. Yes, look at you, love. You're still a prisoner, you stayed there behind with them, locked in that basement. For fifteen years you've done nothing with your life. Not a thing. Look at you, just when we've got the chance to start all over again and you begin to open all the wounds . . . Isn't it time we – ?

PAULINA. Forgot? You're asking me to forget.

GERARDO. Free yourself from them, Paulina, that's what I'm asking.

PAULINA. And let him loose so he can come back in a few years' time?

GERARDO. Let him loose, so he won't come back ever again.

PAULINA. And we see him at the Tavelli and we smile at him, he introduces his lovely wife to us and we smile and we all shake hands and we comment on how warm it is this time of the year and – ?

GERARDO. No need to smile at him but basically yes, that is what we have to do. And start to live, yes.

Brief pause.

PAULINA. Look, Gerardo, I suggest we reach a compromise.

GERARDO. I don't know what you're talking about.

PAULINA. Compromise, an agreement, a negotiation. Everything in this country is done by consensus, isn't it. Isn't that what this transition is all about? They let us have democracy, but they keep control of the economy and of the armed forces? The Commission can investigate the crimes but nobody is punished for them? There's freedom to say anything you want as long as you don't say everything you want?

Brief pause.

So you can see that I'm not that irresponsible or emotional or . . . sick, I propose that we reach an agreement. You want this man freed without bodily harm and I want – would you like to know what I want?

GERARDO. I'd love to know what you want.

PAULINA. When I heard his voice last night, the first thought that rushed through my head, what I've been thinking all these years, when you would catch me with a look that you said was – abstract, fleeting, right? – you know what I was thinking of? Doing to them, systematically, minute by minute, instrument by instrument, what they did to me. Specifically to him, to the doctor . . . Because the others were so vulgar, so ... but he would play Schubert, he would talk about science, he even quoted Nietzsche to me once.

GERARDO. Nietzsche.

PAULINA. I was horrified at myself. That I should have so much hatred inside – but it was the only way to fall asleep at night, the only way of going out with you to cocktail parties in spite of the fact that I couldn't help asking myself if one of the people there wasn't – perhaps not the exact same man, but one of those people might be . . . and so as not to go completely off my rocker and be able to deliver that Tavelli smile you say I'm going to have to continue to deliver – well, I would imagine pushing their head into a bucket of their own shit, or electricity, or when we would be making love and I could feel the possibility of an orgasm building, the very idea of currents going through my body would remind me and then – and then I had to fake it, fake it so you wouldn't know what I was thinking, so you wouldn't feel that it was your failure – oh Gerardo.

GERARDO. Oh, my love, my love.

PAULINA. So when I heard his voice, I thought the only thing I want is to have him raped, have someone fuck him, that's what I thought, that he should know just once what it is to . . . And as I can't rape – I thought that it was a sentence that you would have to carry out.

GERARDO. Don't go on, Paulina.

PAULINA. But then I told myself it would be difficult for you to collaborate in that scheme, after all you do need to have a certain degree of enthusiasm to –

GERARDO. Stop, Paulina.

PAULINA. So I asked myself if we couldn't use a broom. Yes, a broom, Gerardo, you know, a broomstick. But I began to realise that wasn't what I really wanted – something that physical. And you know what conclusion I came to, the only thing I really want?

Brief pause.

I want him to confess. I want him to sit in front of that cassette recorder and tell me what he did – not just to me, everything, to everybody – and then have him write it out in his own handwriting and sign it and I would keep a copy forever – with all the information, the names and data, all the details. That's what I want.

GERARDO. He confesses and you let him go.

PAULINA. I let him go.

GERARDO. And you need nothing more from him?

PAULINA. Not a thing.

Brief pause.

With Miranda's confession in.my hand you'd be safe, you could still be on the Commission and he wouldn't dare send his thugs to harm us because he'd know that if harm came to me or to you, his confession would be all over the newspapers the next day.

GERARDO. And you expect me to believe you that you're going to let him go after he's confessed? You expect him to believe that you won't blow his head off as soon as he's confessed?

PAULINA. I don't see that either of you have an alternative. Look, Gerardo, you need to make this sort of scum afraid. Tell him I hid the car because I'm getting ready to kill him. That the only way to dissuade me is for him to confess. Tell him that nobody knows he came last night, that nobody can ever find him. For his sake, I hope you can convince him.

GERARDO. I have to convince him?

PAULINA. I'd say it's a lot more pleasant than having to fuck him.

GERARDO. There's a problem, of course, you may not have thought of, Paulina. What if he has nothing to confess?

PAULINA. Tell him if he doesn't confess, I'll kill him.

GERARDO. But what if he's not guilty.

PAULINA. I'm in no hurry. Tell him I can wait months for him to confess.

GERARDO. Paulina, you're not listening to me. What can he confess if he's innocent?

PAULINA. If he's innocent? Then he's really screwed.

Lights go down.

Scene Two

Lunch. GERARDO *and* ROBERTO *sit at a table.* ROBERTO *still tied, but this time with his hands in front.* GERARDO *has just finished serving plates of soup.* PAULINA *watches from the terrace. She can see but not hear them.* ROBERTO *and* GERARDO *remain for several silent instants looking at the food.*

GERARDO. You're not hungry, Doctor Miranda?

ROBERTO. Roberto. My name is Roberto. Please treat me with the same familiarity that you – please.

GERARDO. I'd rather speak to you as if you were a client, Doctor Miranda. That will help me out. I think you should eat something.

ROBERTO. I'm not hungry.

GERARDO. Let me . . .

He fills a spoon with soup and feeds ROBERTO *as if he were a baby. During the conversation which follows, he is continually feeding* ROBERTO *and feeding himself:*

ROBERTO. She's mad. You'll have to excuse me for saying this, Gerardo, but your wife . . .

GERARDO. Bread?

ROBERTO. No, thanks.

Brief pause.

She should be receiving some sort of psychiatric treatment for –

GERARDO. To put it brutally, you are her therapy, Doctor.

He cleans ROBERTO's *mouth with a napkin.*

ROBERTO. She's going to kill me.

GERARDO. Unless you confess, she'll kill you.

ROBERTO. But what can I confess? What can I confess if I . . . ?

PAULINA. You may be aware, Doctor, that the secret police used some doctors as – consultants in torture sessions . . .

ROBERTO. The medical association gradually learned of these situations, and looked into them wherever possible.

GERARDO. She is convinced that you are that doctor who . . . And unless you have a way of denying it . . .

ROBERTO. How could I deny it? I'd have to change my voice, prove that this is not my voice – if it's only my voice which damns me, there's no other evidence, nothing that –

GERARDO. And your skin. She mentioned your skin.

ROBERTO. My skin?

GERARDO. And your smell.

ROBERTO. Fantasies of a diseased mind. She could have latched onto any man who came through that door . . .

GERARDO. Unfortunately, you came through that door.

ROBERTO. Look, Gerardo, I'm a quiet man. Anyone can see that I'm incapable of violence – violence of any sort sickens me. I come to my beach house, I wander on the beach, I watch the waves, I hunt for pebbles, I listen to my music – . . .

GERARDO. Schubert?

ROBERTO. Schubert, there's no reason to feel ashamed. I also like Vivaldi and Mozart and Telemann. And I had the stupid idea of bringing Schubert to the beach yesterday. But it was much more stupid to stop for you – Gerardo, I'm in this mess only because I felt sorry for some lunatic waving his arms next to his broken-down car – Look, it's up to you to get me out of here.

GERARDO. I know.

ROBERTO. My ankles hurt, my hands, my back. Couldn't you untie me a little, so –

GERARDO. Roberto, I want to be honest with you. There is only one way to save your life . . .

Brief pause.

I think we have to – indulge her.

ROBERTO. Indulge her?

GERARDO. Humour her, placate her, so she feels that we – that you, are willing to cooperate . . .

ROBERTO. I don't see how I can cooperate, given my rather peculiar position . . .

GERARDO. Indulge her, make her believe that you . . .

ROBERTO. Make her believe that I . . .

GERARDO. She promised me that if you – confessed she would be ready to –

ROBERTO. I haven't got anything to confess!

GERARDO. I think you're going to have to invent something then, because the only way she'll pardon you is if –

ROBERTO (*raises his voice, indignant*). She's got nothing to pardon me for. I did nothing and there's nothing to confess. Do you understand?

Upon hearing ROBERTO*'s voice,* PAULINA *gets up from her seat on the terrace and starts to move toward them.*

Instead of proposing dishonourable solutions to me, you should be out there convincing that madwoman of yours to cease this criminal behaviour before she ruins your career and ends up in jail or in an insane asylum. Tell her that. Or can't you impose a little order in your own house?

GERARDO. Roberto, I –

PAULINA *enters from the terrace.*

PAULINA. Any trouble, darling?

GERARDO. No trouble.

PAULINA. I just saw you a bit . . . agitated.

Brief pause.

Well, I see you've both finished your soup. No one can say I'm not a good cook, can they? Not an ideal housewife? Maybe this ideal housewife should serve you a teensy-weensy cup of coffee, Doctor? Though I believe the doctor here does not drink coffee. Doctor, I am speaking to you. Didn't your mother ever teach you that when –

ROBERTO. Leave my mother out of this. I forbid you to mention my mother.

Brief pause.

PAULINA. I'm sorry to have to agree with you. You're absolutely right. Your mother is not responsible for what you do. I don't know why men always insist on attacking mothers instead of –

Why do they always say son of a bitch, why the bitch instead of the father who taught them in the first place to –

GERARDO. Paulina, would you please do me the favour of leaving so we can continue our conversation? Would you please do me that favour?

PAULINA. That favour and many more. I'll leave you men to fix the world.

She leaves and turns.

Oh, and if he wants to piss, darling, just snap your fingers and I'll come running.

She returns to the same spot on the terrace, watching.

ROBERTO. She's absolutely insane.

GERARDO. When crazy people have power, you've got to indulge them. In her case, a confession –

ROBERTO. But what could a confession – ?

GERARDO. Maybe it liberates her from her phantoms, how can I know what goes on in people's heads after they've been – but I think I understand that need of hers because it coincides with what we were talking about last night, the whole country's need to put into words what happened to us.

ROBERTO. And you?

GERARDO. What about me?

ROBERTO. You. What are you going to do afterwards?

GERARDO. After what?

ROBERTO. You believe her, don't you?

GERARDO. If I thought you were guilty, would I be trying so desperately to save your –

ROBERTO. From the beginning you've been conspiring with her. She plays the bad guy and you play the good guy and –

GERARDO. What do you mean by good –

ROBERTO. Playing roles, she's bad, you're good, to see if you can get me to confess that way. And once I've confessed, you're the one, not her, you're the one who's going to kill me, it's what any man would do, any real man, if they'd raped his wife, it's what I would do if somebody had raped my wife. Cut your balls off. So tell me: you think I'm that fucking doctor, don't you?

Pause. GERARDO *stands up.*

Where are you going?

GERARDO. I'm going to get the gun and blow your fucking brains out. (*Brief pause. Angrier and angrier.*) But first you sonuvabitch I'm going to follow your advice and cut off your balls, you fascist. That's what a real man does, doesn't he. Real macho men blow people's brains out and fuck women when they're tied up on cots. Not like me. I'm a stupid, yellow, soft faggot because I defend the son of a bitch who screwed my wife and destroyed her life. How many times did you screw her? How many times, you bastard?

ROBERTO. Gerardo, I . . . –

GERARDO. Gerardo is gone. I'm here. Me. An eye for an eye is here, a tooth for a tooth, right, isn't that our philosophy?

ROBERTO. I was only joking, it was a –

GERARDO. But on second thoughts, why should I dirty my hands with scum like you –

ROBERTO. – only a joke.

GERARDO. – when there's somebody who'll take much more pleasure in your pain and your death? Why take that one pleasure away from her? I'll call her right away so she can blow your fucking brains out herself.

ROBERTO. Don't go. Don't call her.

GERARDO. I'm tired of being in the middle, in between the two of you. You reach an understanding with her, you convince her.

ROBERTO. Gerardo, I'm scared.

Brief pause. GERARDO *turns around, changes his tone.*

GERARDO. So am I.

ROBERTO. Don't let her kill me.

Brief pause.

What are you going to say to her?

GERARDO. The truth. That you don't want to cooperate.

ROBERTO. I need to know what it is I did, you've got to understand that I don't know what I have to confess. If I were that man, I'd know every – detail, but I don't know anything, right, so . . . if I make a mistake, she'll think I'm – I'll need your help, you'd have to tell me so I can – invent, invent, based on what you tell me.

GERARDO. You're asking me to deceive my wife?

ROBERTO. I'm asking you to save the life of an innocent man,

Escobar. You do believe that I'm innocent, don't you?

GERARDO. You care that much what I believe?

ROBERTO. Of course I do. She isn't the voice of civilisation, you are. She isn't a member of the president's Commission, you are.

GERARDO (*bitter, sad*). No, she isn't . . . Who gives a fuck what she thinks. She's just . . .

He starts to leave.

ROBERTO. Wait. Where are you going? What are you going to say to her?

GERARDO. I'm going to tell her that you need to piss.

Lights go down.

End of Act Two.

ACT THREE

Scene One

Just before evening. PAULINA *and* GERARDO *are outside, on the terrace facing the sea.* ROBERTO *inside, still tied up.* GERARDO *has the cassette recorder on his lap.*

PAULINA. I don't understand why.

GERARDO. I have to know.

PAULINA. Why?

Brief pause.

GERARDO. Paulina, I love you. I need to hear it from your lips. It's not fair that after so many years the person to tell me, ends up being him. It would be – intolerable.

PAULINA. Whereas if I tell you it would be – tolerable.

GERARDO. More tolerable than if he tells me first.

PAULINA. I told this to you already, Gerardo. Wasn't that enough?

GERARDO. Fifteen years ago you started to tell me and then . . .

PAULINA. Did you expect me to keep on talking to you with that bitch there? That bitch came out of your bedroom half naked asking why you were taking so long, and you expected me to –

GERARDO. She wasn't a bitch.

PAULINA. Did she know where I was? Of course she did. A bitch. Fuck a man whose woman wasn't exactly able to defend herself, huh?

GERARDO. We're not going to start all this again, Paulina.

PAULINA. You're the one who started.

GERARDO. How many times do I have to . . . ? – I'd spent two months trying to find you. Then she came by, she said she could help. We had a couple of drinks. My God, I'm also human.

PAULINA. While I defended your life, while your name stayed inside me and never left my mouth – Ask him, ask Miranda if I ever so much as whispered your name, while you . . .

GERARDO. You already forgave me, you forgave me, how many

times will we have to go over this? We'll die from so much
past, so much pain and resentment. Let's finish it – let's finish
that conversation from years ago, let's close this book once and
for all and never speak about it again, never again, never never
again.

PAULINA. Forgive and forget, eh?

GERARDO. Forgive yes, forget, no. But forgive so we can start
again. There's so much to live for, my . . .

PAULINA. What did you want me to do, to talk in front of her? To
tell you, what they did to me, in front of her, that I should – ?
How many times?

GERARDO. How many times what?

PAULINA. How many times did you fuck her?

GERARDO. Paulina . . .

PAULINA. How many?

GERARDO. Baby . . .

PAULINA. How many times did you do it? How many, how
many? I tell you, you tell me.

GERARDO (*desperate, shaking her and then taking her in his
arms*). Paulina, Paulina. You want to destroy me? Is that what
you want?

PAULINA. No.

GERARDO. Well, you're going to destroy me. You're going to
end up in a world where I don't exist, where I won't be here. Is
that what you want?

PAULINA. I want to know how many times you fucked that bitch.

GERARDO. Don't do this to me, Paulina.

PAULINA. That wasn't the first night, was it, Gerardo? You'd
seen her before, right? The truth, Gerardo.

GERARDO. People can die from an excessive dose of the truth,
you know.

PAULINA. How many times, Gerardo. You tell me, I tell you.

GERARDO. Twice.

PAULINA. That night. What about before that night?

GERARDO (*very low*). Three times.

PAULINA. What?

GERARDO (*raising his voice*). Three times.

PAULINA. She was that good? You liked her that much? And she liked it too. She must have really enjoyed it if she came back for –

GERARDO. Do you understand what you're doing to me?

PAULINA. Beyond repair, huh? Irreparable.

GERARDO (*desperate*). What more do you want from me? We survived the dictatorship, we survived, and now we're going to do to each other what those bastards out there couldn't do to us? You want that?

PAULINA (*quietly*). No.

GERARDO. You want me to leave? Is that what you want? You want me to go out that door and never see you again? Good God, is that what you want?

PAULINA. No.

GERARDO. That's what you're going to get.

Brief pause.

I'm in your hands like a baby, I've got no defences, I'm naked in front of you like the day I was born. You want to treat me like you treat the man who –

PAULINA. No.

GERARDO. You want me to . . . ?

PAULINA (*murmuring*). I want you. You. I want you inside me, alive. I want you making love to me without ghosts in bed and I want you on the Commission defending the truth and I want you in the air I breathe and I want you in my Schubert that I can start listening to again –

GERARDO. Yes, Paulina, yes, yes.

PAULINA. – and I want us adopting a child and I want to care for you minute by minute like you took care of me after that night –

GERARDO. Never mention that bitch of a night again. If you go on and on about that night, you'll – kill me. Is that what you want?

PAULINA. No.

GERARDO. Are you going to tell me then?

PAULINA. Yes.

GERARDO. Everything?

PAULINA. Everything.

GERARDO. That's the way, that's how we'll get out of this mess – without hiding a thing from each other, together.

PAULINA. That's the way.

GERARDO. I'm going to turn on the recorder. You don't mind, love, if I turn it on?

PAULINA. Turn it on.

GERARDO *turns it on.*

GERARDO. Just as if you were sitting in front of the Commission.

PAULINA. I don't know how to begin.

GERARDO. Begin with your name.

PAULINA. My maiden name is Paulina Salas. Now I am married to Gerardo Escobar, the lawyer, but at that time –

GERARDO. Date.

PAULINA. April 6th, 1975, I was single. I was walking along San Antonio Street –

GERARDO. Be as precise as you can.

PAULINA. – at about two-fifteen in the afternoon, and when I reached the corner at Huérfanos Street behind me I heard – three men got out of a car, one of them stuck a gun in my back, 'One word and we'll blow you away, Miss.' He spat the words into my ear – he had garlic on his breath. I was surprised that I should focus on such an insignificant detail, the lunch he had eaten, begin to think about how he was digesting that food with all the organs that I had been studying in anatomy class. Later on I'd reproach myself, I would have lots of time to think about it, why didn't I call out, I knew that if that happened you're supposed to scream, so people can know who is – call out your name, I'm Paulina Salas, they're kidnapping me, if you don't scream out that first moment you're already defeated, and I submitted too easily, obeyed them right away without even a gesture of defiance. All my life, I've always been much too obedient.

The lights begin to go down.

The doctor wasn't among them. I met Doctor Miranda for the first time three days later when . . . That's when I met Doctor Miranda.

The lights go down further and PAULINA's *voice continues in the darkness, only the cassette recorder lit by the light of the moon.*

At first, I thought he would save me. He was so soft, so – nice,

after what the others had done to me. And then, all of a sudden,
I heard a Schubert quartet. There is no way of describing what
it means to hear that wonderful music in the darkness, when
you haven't eaten for the last three days, when your body is
falling apart, when . . .

In the darkness, we hear ROBERTO'*s voice overlapping
with* PAULINA'*s and the second movement of* Death and the
Maiden.

ROBERTO'S VOICE. I would put on the music because it helped
me in my role, the role of good guy, as they call it, I would put
on Schubert because it was a way of gaining the prisoners'
trust. But I also knew it was a way of alleviating their suffering.
You've got to believe it was a way of alleviating the prisoners'
suffering. Not only the music, but everything else I did. That's
how they approached me, at first.

*The lights go up as if the moon were coming out. It is night-
time.* ROBERTO *is in front of the cassette recorder, confessing.
The Schubert fades.*

The prisoners were dying on them, they told me, they needed
someone to help care for them, someone they could trust. I've
got a brother, who was a member of the secret services. You
can pay the communists back for what they did to Dad, he told
me one night – my father had a heart attack the day the peasants
took over his land at Las Toltecas. The stroke paralysed him –
he lost his capacity for speech, would spend hours simply
looking at me, his eyes said, Do something. But that's not why
I accepted. The real real truth, it was for humanitarian reasons.
We're at war, I thought, they want to kill me and my family,
they want to install a totalitarian dictatorship, but even so, they
still have the right to some form of medical attention. It was
slowly, almost without realising how, that I became involved in
more delicate operations, they let me sit in on sessions where
my role was to determine if the prisoners could take that much
torture, that much electric current. At first I told myself that it
was a way of saving people's lives, and I did, because many
times I told them – without it being true, simply to help the
person who was being tortured – I ordered them to stop or the
prisoner would die. But afterwards I began to – bit by bit, the
virtue I was feeling turned into excitement – the mask of virtue
fell off it and it, the excitement, it hid, it hid, it hid from me
what I was doing, the swamp of what – By the time Paulina
Salas was brought in it was already too late. Too late.

The lights start to slowly go down.

RO8BERTO: . . . too late. A kind of – brutalisation took over my
life, I began to really truly like what I was doing. It became a

game. My curiosity was partly morbid, partly scientific. How much can this woman take? More than the other one? How's her sex? Does her sex dry up when you put the current through her? Can she have an orgasm under those circumstances? She is entirely in your power, you can carry out all your fantasies, you can do what you want with her.

The lights continue to fade while ROBERTO's *voice speaks on in the semi-darkness, a beam of moonlight on the cassette recorder.*

Everything they have forbidden you since ever, whatever your mother ever urgently whispered you were never to do. You begin to dream with her, with all those women. Come on, Doctor, they would say to me, you're not going to refuse free meat, are you, one of them would sort of taunt me. His name was – they called him Stud – a nickname, because I never found out his real name. They like it, Doctor, Stud would say to me – all these bitches like it and if you put on that sweet little music of yours, they'll get even cosier. He would say this in front of the women, in front of Paulina Salas he would say it, and finally I, finally I – but not one ever died on me, not one of the women, not one of the men.

The lights go up and it is now dawning. ROBERTO, *untied, writes on a sheet of paper his own words from the cassette recorder. In front of him, many sheets of handwritten pages.* PAULINA *and* GERARDO *watch him.*

ROBERTO'S VOICE (*from the recorder*). As far as I can remember, I took part in the – interrogation of ninety-four prisoners, including Paulina Salas. It is all I can say. I ask forgiveness.

GERARDO *switches off the cassette recorder while* ROBERTO *writes.*

ROBERTO. – forgiveness.

GERARDO *switches the cassette recorder back on.*

ROBERTO'S VOICE. And I hope that this confession proves that I feel real repentance and that just as the country is reaching reconciliation and peace . . .

GERARDO *switches off the cassette recorder.*

GERARDO. Did you write that? Just as the country is reaching reconciliation and peace?

He switches it on again.

ROBERTO'S VOICE. – so too should I be allowed to live the rest of my days with my terrible secret. There can be no worse punishment than that which is imposed upon me by the voice of my conscience.

ROBERTO (*while he writes*). – punishment . . . my conscience.

GERARDO *switches off the cassette recorder. A moment's silence.*

And now what? You want me to sign?

PAULINA. First write there that this is all done of your own free will, without any sort of pressure whatsoever.

ROBERTO. That's not true.

PAULINA. You want real pressure, Doctor?

ROBERTO *writes down a couple of phrases, shows them to* GERARDO, *who moves his head affirmatively.* ROBERTO *signs.* PAULINA *looks at the signature, collects the paper, takes the cassette out of the recorder, puts another cassette in, pushes a button. We hear* ROBERTO's *confession on the tape.*

ROBERTO'S VOICE (*on tape*). I would put on the music because it helped me in my role, the role of good guy, as they call it, I would put on Schubert because it was a way of gaining the prisoners' trust. But I also knew it was a way of alleviating their suffering.

GERARDO. Paulina. It's over.

ROBERTO'S VOICE (*on tape*). You've got to believe it was a way of alleviating the prisoners' suffering.

GERARDO (*turning off the cassette recorder*). It is over.

PAULINA. Almost over, yes.

GERARDO. So don't you think it's about time we . . .

PAULINA. Right. We had an agreement.

She stands up, goes to the window, breathes in the air of the sea deeply.

To think that I would spend hours here like this, at dawn, trying to make out the things left behind by the tide during the night, staring at those shapes, wondering what they were, if they would be dragged out to sea again. And now . . . And now . . .

GERARDO. Paulina!

PAULINA (*turning suddenly*). I'm glad to see that you're still a man of principle. I thought I'd have to convince you now, now that you know he really is guilty, I thought I'd have to convince you not to kill him.

GERARDO. I wouldn't stain my soul with someone like him.

PAULINA (*throws him the keys to the car*). Right. Go and get his car.

Brief pause.

GERARDO. And I can leave him alone with you?

PAULINA. Wouldn't you say I'm old enough?

Brief pause.

GERARDO. All right, all right, I'll go get the car . . . Take care of yourself.

PAULINA. You too.

GERARDO *goes toward the door.*

PAULINA. Oh – and don't forget to give his jack back.

GERARDO (*trying to smile*). And don't you forget to return his Schubert cassette. You've got your own.

He exits. PAULINA *watches him leave.* ROBERTO *unties his ankles.*

ROBERTO. If you wouldn't mind, I would like to go to the bathroom. I suppose there is no reason why you should continue to accompany me?

PAULINA. Don't move, Doctor. There's still a little matter pending.

Brief pause.

It's going to be an incredibly beautiful day. You know the only thing that's missing now, Doctor, the one thing I need to make this day really truly perfect?

Brief pause .

To kill you. So I can listen to my Schubert without thinking that you'll also be listening to it, soiling my day and my Schubert and my country and my husband. That's what I need . . .

ROBERTO. Madam, your husband left here trusting that you – you gave your word . . .

PAULINA. But when I gave my word – I still had a doubt – a teensy-weensy doubt – that you really were that man. Because Gerardo was right, in his way. Proof, hard proof – well, I could have been mistaken. But I knew that if you confessed – and when I heard you, my last doubts vanished. Now that I know, now that you are that man, I could not live in peace with myself and let you live.

She points the gun at him.

You have a minute to pray, Doctor.

ROBERTO *slowly stands.*

ROBERTO. Don't do it. I'm innocent.

PAULINA. You've confessed.

ROBERTO. That confession, ma'am . . . It's false.

PAULINA. What do you mean, false?

ROBERTO. I made it up. We made it up.

PAULINA. It seemed quite true to me, painfully familiar as far as I'm concerned . . .

ROBERTO. Your husband told me what to write, I invented some of it, some of it was invented by me, but most of it was what he got from you, from what he knew had happened to you, so you'd let me go, he convinced me that it was the only way that you wouldn't kill me and I had to – you must know how, under pressure, we say anything, but I'm innocent, Mrs. Escobar, God in Heaven knows that –

PAULINA. Do not invoke God, Doctor, when you are so close to finding out whether He exists or not. Stud.

ROBERTO. What?

PAULINA. Several times in your confession you mention Stud. He must have been a large man, muscular, he bit his fingernails, right, he bit his goddamn fingernails. Stud.

ROBERTO. I never met anyone like the man you're describing. The name was given to me by your husband. Everything I said comes from what your husband helped me to invent. Ask him when he comes back.

PAULINA. I don't need to ask him. I knew that he'd do that, I knew he'd use my words for your confession. That's the sort of person he is. He always thinks that he's more intelligent than everybody else, he always thinks that he's got to save somebody. I don't blame him. That's why I love him. We lied to each other out of love. He deceived me for my own good. I deceived him for his own good. But I'm the one who came out on top in this game. I gave him the name Bud, Doctor, I gave him the wrong name, to see if you would correct it. And you did correct it. You corrected the name Bud and you substituted the name Stud and if you were innocent –

ROBERTO. I'm telling you it was your husband who – Listen. Please listen. He must have thought Stud was the name a man like that would – I don't know why he – Ask him. Ask him.

PAULINA. It's not the only correction that you made. There were other. . . lies.

ROBERTO. What lies, what lies?

PAULINA. – small lies, small variations, that I inserted in my story to Gerardo, and you corrected most of them. It turned out just as I planned. You were so scared that if you didn't get it right . . . But I'm not going to kill you because you're guilty, Doctor, but because you haven't repented at all. I can only forgive someone who really repents, who stands up amongst those he has wronged and says, I did this, I did it, and I'll never do it again.

ROBERTO. What more do you want? You've got more than all the victims in this country will ever get.

He gets down on his knees.

What more do you want?

PAULINA. The truth, Doctor. The truth and I'll let you go. Repent and I'll let you go. You have ten seconds. One, two, three, four, five, six. Time is running out. Seven. Say it!

ROBERTO *stands up.*

ROBERTO. No. I won't. Because even if I confess, you'll never be satisfied. You're going to kill me anyway. So go ahead and kill me. I'm not going to let any sick woman treat me like this. If you want to kill me, do it. But you're killing an innocent man.

PAULINA. Eight.

ROBERTO. So someone did terrible things to you and now you're doing something terrible to me and tomorrow somebody else is going to – on and on and on. I have children, two boys, a girl. Are they supposed to spend the next fifteen years looking for you until they find you? And then –

PAULINA. Nine.

ROBERTO. Oh Paulina – isn't it time we stopped?

PAULINA. And why does it always have to be people like me who have to sacrifice, why are we always the ones who have to make concessions when something has to be conceded, why always me who has to bite her tongue, why? Well, not this time. This time I am going to think about myself, about what I need. If only to do justice in one case, just one. What do we lose? What do we lose by killing one of them? What do we lose? What do we lose?

They freeze in their positions as the lights begin to go down slowly. We begin to hear music from the last movement of Mozart's Dissonant Quartet. *PAULINA and ROBERTO are covered from view by a giant mirror which descends, forcing*

*the members of the audience to look at themselves. For a few
minutes, the Mozart quartet is heard, while the spectators
watch themselves in the mirror. Selected slowly moving spots
flicker over the audience, picking out two or three at a time, up
and down rows.*

Scene Two

A concert hall. An evening some months later. GERARDO *and*
PAULINA *appear, elegantly dressed. They sit down facing the
mirror, their backs to the spectators, perhaps in two chairs or in
two of the seats in the audience itself. Under the music we can
hear typical sounds of an audience during a concert: throats
clearing, an occasional cough, the ruffling of programme notes,
even some heavy breathing. When the music ends,* GERARDO
*begins to applaud and we can hear the applause growing from
what is an invisible public.* PAULINA *does not applaud. The
applause begins to die down and then we hear the habitual sounds
that come from a concert hall when the first part of a programme
is over: more throat clearing, murmurs, bodies shuffling toward
the foyer. They both begin to go out, greeting people, stopping to
chat for an instant. They slowly distance themselves from their
seats and advance along an imaginary foyer which is apparently
full of spectators. We hear mutterings, etc.* GERARDO *begins to
talk to members of the audience, as if they were at the concert.
His words can be heard above the murmurs of the public.*

GERARDO (*intimately, talking to diverse spectators*). Why, thank
    you, thank you so much . . . Well, I am a bit tired, but it was
    worth it . . . Yes, we're very pleased with the Final Report of
    the Commission.

*PAULINA slowly leaves him, going to one side where a small
bar has been installed.* GERARDO *continues speaking with his
audience until she returns .*

People are acting with enormous generosity, without the hint of
seeking a personal vendetta . . . Well, I always knew that our
work would help in the process of healing, but I was surprised
it would start on the very first day we convened. An old woman
came in to testify. The woman was so timid. She began to speak
standing up. 'Please sit down,' the president of the Commission
said and stood up to hold her chair for her. She sat down and
began to sob. Then she looked at us and said: 'This is the first
time, sir,' she said to us – her husband had disappeared fourteen
years ago, and she had spent thousands of hours petitioning,

thousands of hours waiting – 'This is the first time,' she said to us, 'in all these years, sir, that somebody asks me to sit down.' It was the first time that anyone had ever asked her to sit down.

Meanwhile, PAULINA *has bought some candy – and as she pays,* ROBERTO *enters, under a light which has a faint phantasmagoric moonlight quality. He could be real or he could be an illusion in* PAULINA's *head.* PAULINA *does not see him yet. A bell goes off to indicate that the concert is about to recommence. She returns to* GERARDO's *side who, by this time, should be finishing his monologue.* ROBERTO *stays behind, watching* PAULINA *and* GERARDO *from a distance.*

As for the murderers, even if we do not know or cannot reveal their names – ah, Paulie, just in time. Well, I'll see you later, old man. Now I've finally got some free time. Maybe we could have a couple of drinks at home. Pau mixes a margarita that'll stand your hair on end.

GERARDO *and* PAULINA *sit in their seats.* ROBERTO *goes to another seat, always looking at* PAULINA. *Applause is heard when the imaginary musicians come on. The instruments are tested and tuned. Then* Death and the Maiden *begins.* GERARDO *looks at* PAULINA, *who looks forward. He takes her hand and then also begins to look forward. After a few instants, she turns slowly and looks at* ROBERTO. *Their eyes interlock for a moment. Then she turns her head and faces the stage and the mirror. The lights go down while the music plays and plays and plays.*

Curtain .

AFTERWORD

Eight or nine years ago, when General Augusto Pinochet was still the dictator of Chile and I was still in exile, I began tentatively exploring in my mind a dramatic situation that was someday to become the core of *Death and the Maiden*. A man whose car breaks down on the highway is given a lift home by a friendly stranger. The man's wife, believing she recognises in the stranger the voice of the torturer who raped her some years before, kidnaps him and decides to put him on trial. On several occasions I sat down to scribble what I then imagined would be a novel. A few hours and a couple of unsatisfactory pages later, I would give up in frustration. Something essential was missing. I could not figure out, for instance, who the woman's husband was, how he would react to her violence, if he would believe her. Nor were the historical circumstances under which the story developed clear to me, the symbolic and secret connections to the larger life of the country itself, the world beyond the narrow, claustrophobic boundaries of that woman's home. The use of a forceps may be necessary to ensure the birth of a child that needs help out of the womb, but I had by then blessedly learned that when characters do not want to be born, forceps may scar them and twist their lives irreparably. My trio would, unfortunately, have to wait.

They were forced to wait a long time. It was not until Chile returned to democracy in 1990 and I myself therefore returned to resettle there with my family after seventeen years of exile, that I finally understood how the story had to be told.

My country was at the time (and still is now as I write this) living an uneasy transition to democracy, with Pinochet no longer the president but still in command of the armed forces, still able to threaten another coup if people became unruly or, more specifically, if attempts were made to punish the human rights violations of the outgoing regime. And in order to avoid chaos and constant confrontation, the new government had to find a way of not alienating Pinochet supporters who continued occupying significant areas of power in the judiciary, the senate, the town councils – and particularly the economy. In the area of human rights, our democratically elected president, Patricio Aylwin, responded to this quandary by naming a Commission – called the Rettig Commission, after the eighty-year-old lawyer who headed it – that would investigate the crimes of the dictatorship that had ended in death or its presumption, but which would neither name the perpetrators nor judge them. This was an important step toward healing a sick country: the truth of the terror unleashed upon us that we had always known in a private and fragmented fashion would finally receive public recognition, established forever as official history, recreating a community fractured by divisions and hatred that we wished to leave behind. On the other hand, justice would not be done and the traumatic experience of hundreds of thousands of other victims, those who had survived, would not even be addressed. Aylwin was steering a prudent but valiant course between those who wanted past terror totally buried and those who wanted it totally revealed.

As I watched with fascination how the Commission carried out its difficult task, it slowly dawned on me that here might be the key to the unresolved story that had been buzzing inside my head for so many years: that fictitious kidnapping and trial should occur, not in a nation under the boot of a dictator, but in one that was in transition to democracy, where so many Chileans were grappling with the hidden traumas of what had been done to them while other Chileans wondered if their crimes would now be revealed. It also became clear that the way to make the husband of the tortured woman have a tremendous stake in the outcome of that kidnapping was to make him a member of a commission similar to the one headed by Rettig. And it did not take me long to conclude that, rather than a novel, what needed to be written was a play.

It was a risky idea. I knew from experience that distance is often the best ally of an author and that when we deal with events that are being enacted and multiplied in immediate history, a danger always exists of succumbing to a 'documentary' or overly realistic approach, losing universality and creative freedom, trying to adjust the characters to the events unfolding around us rather than letting them emerge on their own, letting them surprise and disturb us. I also knew that I would be savagely criticised by some in my own country for 'rocking the boat' by reminding everyone about the long-term effects of terror and violence on people precisely at a time when we were being asked to be notably cautious.

I felt, however, that if as a citizen I had to be responsible and reasonable, as an artist I had to answer the wild mating call of my characters and break the silence which was weighing upon so many of my self-censored compatriots, fearful of creating 'trouble' for the new democracy. It was then and is now more than ever my belief that a fragile democracy is strengthened by expressing for all to see the deep dramas and sorrows and hopes that underlie its existence and that it is not by hiding the damage we have inflicted on ourselves that we will avoid its repetition.

As I began to write I found the characters trying to figure out the sort of questions that so many Chileans were asking themselves privately, but that hardly anyone seemed interested in posing in public. How can those who tortured and those who were tortured co-exist in the same land? How to heal a country that has been traumatised by repression if the fear to speak out is still omnipresent everywhere? And how do you reach the truth if lying has become a habit? How do we keep the past alive without becoming its prisoner? How do we forget it without risking its repetition in the future? Is it legitimate to sacrifice the truth to ensure peace? And what are the consequences of suppressing that past and the truth it is whispering or howling to us? Are people free to search for justice and equality if the threat of a military intervention haunts them? And given these circumstances, can violence be avoided? And how guilty are we all of what happened to those who suffered most? And perhaps the greatest dilemma of them all: how to confront these issues without destroying the national consensus, which creates democratic stability?

Three weeks later, *Death and the Maiden* was ready.

If the play revealed many of the hidden conflicts that were just under the surface of the nation, and therefore posed a clear threat to people's psychological security, it could also be an instrument through which we explored our identity and the contradictory options available to us in the years to come.

A multitude of messages of the contemporary imagination, specifically those that are channelled through the mass entertainment media, assure us, over and over, that there is an easy, even facile, comforting, answer to most of our problems. Such an aesthetic strategy seems to me not only to falsify and disdain human experience but in the case of Chile or of any country that is coming out of a period of enormous conflict and pain, it turns out to be counterproductive for the community, freezing its maturity and growth. I felt that *Death and the Maiden* touched upon a tragedy in an almost Aristotelian sense, a work of art that might help a collective to purge itself, through pity and terror, in other words to force the spectators to confront those predicaments that, if not brought into the light of day, could lead to their ruin.

Which is a way of stating that this piece of fiction, as so much of what I had written previously in my novels, stories, poems, and other plays, was not merely Chilean in scope but addressed problems that could be found all over the world, all over the twentieth century, all over the face of humanity through the ages. It was not only about a country that is afraid and simultaneously needful of understanding its fear and its scars, not only about the long-term effects of torture and violence on human beings and the beautiful body of their land, but about other themes that have always obsessed me: what happens when women take power. How can you tell the truth if the mask you have adopted ends up being identical to your face? How does memory beguile and save and guide us? How can we keep our innocence once we have tasted evil? How to forgive those who have hurt us irreparably? How do we find a language that is political but not pamphletary? How to tell stories that are both popular and ambiguous, stories that can be understood by large audiences and yet contain stylistic experimentation, that are mythical and also about immediate human beings?

Death and the Maiden appears in English at a moment when humanity is undergoing extraordinary changes, when there is great hope for the future and great confusion about what that future may bring. In the current debate, little is being heard from that submerged zone of our species who live far from the centres of power but are often near the quick centre of suffering where ethical choices determine the immediate shape of things to come and things to be postponed. In times such as these, when the more miserable and distant lands seem to disappear from the horizon, it may help us a bit, perhaps a teensy-weensy bit, I would hope, to think of the Paulinas, the Gerardos, the Robertos, of the world – to figure out for ourselves which of these three we most resemble, how much of our secluded lives are expressed in each of these characters and in all of them. Until finally, I would also hope, we would realise that what we feel when we watch and whisper and ache with these faraway people from faraway Chile could well be that strange trembling state of humanity we call recognition, a bridge across our divided globe.

Ariel Dorfman,
11 September 1991